Series title:

BLACK LEADERS IN THE FREEDOM STRUGGLE

FREDERICK DOUGLASS

by Marie Stuart

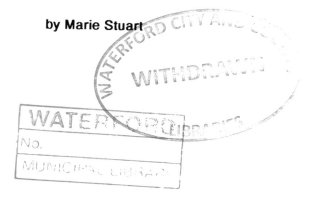

Illustrated by Folake Shoga

This book is part of a series written by Marie Stuart (Tyrwhitt) and published in her memory.

Marie wanted stories about the lives of these brave people to be more widely known. She believed that such stories would serve to encourage those facing the same challenges today.

Published in 1990 by Central and East Bristol Adult Continuing Education©, Alexandra Park Centre, Alexandra Park, Bristol BS16 2BG with the sponsorship of the County of Avon and relatives, friends and colleagues of Marie Tyrwhitt.

Reprinted in 1995 by the same group now known as ©Marie Tyrwhitt Publications at Stoke Lodge Community Education Centre, Stoke Lodge, Shirehampton Road, Stoke Bishop, Bristol BS9 1BN.

Reprinted 2001

Computer generated text and artwork by Alan Bain, 14 Tyndall's Park Road, Bristol BS8 1PY.

Printed by University of the West of England, Bristol Printing and Stationery Services.

FREDERICK DOUGLASS
Chapter 1. Life on the Great Home Farm

Frederick Douglass was born in Maryland in the U.S.A. in the year 1817. His mother was a black slave named Harriet Bailey. His father was white. Fred never knew him, and he only saw his mother three or four times when he was very young. She worked on a plantation twelve miles away from the farm where he lived, and she had to walk there after a hard day's work. She could only come at night and see him when he was in bed. She died when he was about seven years old.

Fred lived with his grandmother in a house on the edge of the plantation. Fred's younger brother and sister lived there, as well as a lot of other children whose mothers were slaves. His grandmother was kind to them, but she did not have much food to give them, and they ran about with no shoes and often no clothes. None of them knew when it was their birthday. Fred was sad about that because all the white children could tell how old they were. Also, they got presents on their birthday, but the black children never had presents.

He must have been about seven years old when he left his grandmother and started to work for his first master, Captain Anthony. The captain owned two or three farms and about thirty slaves. His overseer was a cruel drunkard who always carried a cow-skin strap and a heavy cudgel.

One day Fred saw him beating his Aunt Hester because she had gone out with a young man without asking him if she could. He made her take off her clothes as far as her waist. Then he tied her hands together and led her to a stool under a large hook in an overhead beam. He put the rope over the hook so that she had to stand on her toes. Then he whipped her naked back with the cow-hide strap until she was covered with blood. Fred was so horrified by what he saw and by the screams of his aunt that he never forgot it.

Captain Anthony had two sons, Andrew and Richard, and a daughter, Lucretia, who was married to Captain Thomas Auld. They all lived in a big house on the home-plantation of Colonel Edward Lloyd. Fred spent the next two years of his life on this plantation, working with the other slaves in the fields. The crops they grew were tobacco, corn (or maize) and wheat. When it was harvested it was taken by river to Baltimore in a sloop manned by four slaves and Captain Thomas Auld, Lucretia's husband.

Colonel Lloyd had between three and four hundred slaves on his home-plantation and he owned many more elsewhere. He was a very rich man. His home-farm was like a big business place. It was also like a magistrates court. If a slave did something wrong or tried to run away, he was brought there and whipped publicly as a warning to the other slaves.

They had to go there to get their food and clothes. The monthly allowance of food was:

Eight pounds of pork or fish; One bushel of corn meal.

The yearly clothes hand-out was:

Two coarse linen shirts; One pair of linen trousers, for summer; One pair of coarse canvas trousers, for winter; One jacket; One pair of stockings; One pair of shoes.

The allowance for the slave children was given to their mothers. Those too young to work had only two coarse linen shirts, the same for boys and girls. In fact, the children were almost naked for all seasons of the year.

There were no beds, and only one coarse blanket, and these only for the men and women. They slept on the floor, old and young, married and single, all in the same room. They were wakened at dawn by the overseer's horn. He would stand at the door with a large stick and cow-skin strap ready to whip anyone who was late. He would whip the mothers in front of their crying children, shouting at them to hurry up.

The home-plantation of Colonel Lloyd was a very busy place. There was a smithy where the horses were shod, and mills where corn was ground. There were looms for weaving the coarse cloth, and carpenters' benches and tools where cartwrights made waggons and casks for holding beer. In fact it was a kind of village, only all the people who did the work there were slaves. They got no pay and were always under the eye of the overseer and within the reach of his whip.

It was called the Great House Farm by the slaves who worked on the out-farms. They were always glad when they were chosen to go there to collect the monthly allowance for themselves and their fellow-slaves. While on their way through the woods they would start singing:

"We're going to the Great House Farm,

O, yea! O yea! O!"

But Fred could always hear the sadness in their voices as they sang.

Besides the fields where the crops grew, Colonel Lloyd also had a beautiful garden, full of all kinds of fruit: apples, pears, oranges and plums. But if one of the slave boys was tempted to pick one, he was whipped by the head gardener. Also, the fence round the garden was painted with tar, so that if a boy was seen with tar on his trousers he was whipped. Colonel Lloyd had three sons and three sons-in-law and each of them could whip the slaves, so it was not easy to escape the lash.

Colonel Lloyd kept horses, and he seemed to care more for them than for the two slaves, a father and his son, who looked after them. Fred says that he often saw the Colonel make old Barney, the father, uncover his bald head and kneel down on the cold, damp ground "to receive upon his toil-worn shoulders more than thirty lashes at a time for the slightest neglect, or imagined neglect."

Yet the slaves seldom complained. Who was there to complain to? And if the Master heard a man complain, he could sell him to a slave-trader with no warning, so that the poor slave would be forever separated from his family and friends. Because of this, slaves always said that they were being well treated if they were asked about their master.

Fred tells about one man who ran away during a whipping and jumped into a nearby stream. The overseer ordered him to come back, saying that he would give him three calls to obey. The slave did not obey, and the overseer shot him dead on the spot. He gave this as an excuse that if one slave disobeyed, the others would do the same. So he was not brought to court or punished in any way.

Fred lived on Colonel Lloyd's plantation until he was about eight years old. He himself was not whipped, and only suffered from cold and hunger. His food was always the same, coarse corn boiled into 'mush'. It was put in a large wooden trough and set down on the ground. Then the children were called to come and eat "like so many pigs". They had no spoons but used oyster shells, or flat pebbles, or their bare hands. Those who ate the fastest got the most.

Chapter 2. "I will learn to Read and Write!"

After he left Colonel Lloyd, Fred was sent to Baltimore as a home-servant in the house of Mr. Hugh Auld. He was glad to go, and wondered why he had been chosen. Was it because Captain Anthony, his first master, was really his father? He knew that Captain Anthony had three legal children, much older than Fred himself. One of them was Lucretia, who was married to Captain Thomas Auld. Mr. Hugh Auld was this man's brother, and as he did not own any other slaves perhaps he would be kinder.

Fred sailed to Baltimore in the sloop with Master Thomas, who was the Captain. When he got to the house it seemed as if his dream was coming true. He was met at the door by Mr. and Mrs. Auld and their little son, Thomas. "And here," he says, "I saw what I had never seen before, a white face beaming with the most kindly emotions! It was the face of my new mistress, Sophie Auld. I wish I could describe the rapture that flooded through my soul as I beheld it ... Little Thomas was told that I was *his* Freddy, and I was told to take care of Little Thomas."

Mrs. Auld had never owned a slave before her marriage and so, as she was a kind woman by nature, she treated Fred as she would treat a little eight-year-old white boy. He, for his part, did not know how to behave towards her. She did not like him to crouch in front of her, and did not think he was rude if he looked in her face when he spoke to her.

She began to teach him his ABC and to read words of three letters, like 'cat' and 'dog'. But when Mr. Auld found out what she was doing he was very cross. He told his wife that it was unlawful, as well as unsafe, to teach a slave to read: "A nigger should know nothing but to obey his master - to do as he is told," he said. He forbade her to go on teaching Fred to read.

His words had the opposite effect on Fred from what he had intended. From that moment the slave boy made up his mind to learn to read, even though he now had no teacher. "In learning to read, I owe almost as much to the bitter opposition of my master as to the kindly aid of my mistress," he wrote. Child as he was, he saw the importance of education.

Fred lived in Master Hugh's house for seven years, during which time he learned both to read and write. His mistress refused to teach him or to let anyone else do so. She no longer treated him as a little boy but as one of her belongings. He said later that slavery was as damaging to her as it was to him. But how could he learn without a teacher? He made friends with all the white children he met in the street when he was sent on an errand. By running, he was able to do the errand quickly and find time to get a 'lesson' from one of his friends on his return. He 'paid' them with a piece of bread, for he could always get this at home, and the white children were always hungry; but, being white, they could go to school.

One day, he got hold of a book and read what someone had written about slavery. The more he read, the more angry he felt. The thought of being a slave all his life made him very sad. Then he heard someone talking about 'Abolitionists'. At first he did not know what the word meant. Then he got a piece of paper which had been signed by a lot of people in the North asking for the 'Abolition of Slavery'. He wanted to find out more about it but there was no one he could ask.

However, one day when he was on the wharf he saw two Irishmen unloading stones from one of the ships. He went to help them, and when they thanked him they asked if he was a slave for life. When he said "yes," they told him to run away to the North where he would be free. As he was only about twelve years old, he knew he was too young to do anything yet. But he made up his mind that one day he would try. That meant he must first learn to write, since the time might come when he would need to write his own 'pass'.

In the shipyard he saw that after the carpenters had cut a piece of timber they wrote a mark on it to show in which part of the ship it was going to be used. The marks were letters of the alphabet, such as 'S' for 'Starboard'.

He was soon able to copy them. Then he 'dared' the white boys who had taught him to read, to write them better than he could. They were proud to show off their skill in writing, and in this way Fred got a lot of 'lessons'. As he had no pen or paper he used any handy board-fence, brick wall or pavement, and a lump of chalk.

By this time, his little master, Thomas, was going to school and learning to write. He used to bring home his copy-books to show his parents, for them to admire and praise him. The books were then put aside and forgotten, but not by Fred. When the Mistress was at a Women's Meeting on Monday afternoons, leaving him in charge of the house, he used to spend the time writing in the empty spaces left in these books by Master Thomas. So, by the time he was ten years old, he was able to write well.

Chapter 3. Life Becomes Much Harder

Then life changed for him once more, because Captain Anthony, his first master, died. Fred had still belonged to him, although he was working for Hugh Auld.

Fred was sent back to the place of his birth to be valued. All of the slaves were put together, men and women, old and young, married and single - with the horses, sheep and pigs. When the valuers had decided how much each slave or each animal was worth, Captain Anthony's son or daughter, who had inherited them, shared them out between them. The slaves of course had no say in the matter.

They all feared being owned by Andrew, the son who had a bad temper, but Fred was given to the daughter, Lucretia, and she sent him back to Hugh Auld, who was her brother-in-law. However, Lucretia died soon afterwards, and her husband, Thomas Auld, claimed Fred back. When he was with Master Hugh, Fred had always had enough to eat, but Thomas Auld was mean as well as cruel. Now Fred was always hungry. At fifteen, he was growing fast and needed plenty of food. (As a fully grown man he was over six feet tall and powerfully built). What made it worse was that as he worked in the kitchen with his sister and aunt he saw all the good food which was being served to the many visitors who came to the house. The left-over food was locked away "to moulder in the safe and smoke-house" rather than be given to the hungry slaves. This made Fred mad!

He was far too outspoken for Master Thomas and was given many severe beatings. In the end, he was sent away to a Mr. Covey, a farm-renter, who was famous for 'breaking' young slaves who were rebellious. So, on January 1st 1833, Fred, now a strong young man of sixteen, went to live with Mr. Covey.

Mr. Covey was really a poor white man who worked on the rented farm himself . He did not own the slaves who were sent to him by their masters to make sure they worked hard. They had to work in all weathers from dawn till sundown.

During his first six months there, Fred said that he "tasted the bitter dregs of slavery". Sunday was his only free day, and sometimes he would walk to a spot where he could overlook Chesapeake Bay and see the white sails of ships from all over the world. How he longed to escape in one of them! He dreamed of running away, but knew he must wait till he was older.

Then, one day in August, he was working with three other slaves threshing wheat. His job was to carry the heavy stooks to the fan. Suddenly he was overcome by the heat and fell down. It was probably sunstroke. The work had to stop and Mr. Covey came over to find out why. He whipped Fred to force him to get up, but he couldn't. At last he managed to crawl away and hide in some bushes.

He made up his mind to go to Master Thomas and make a complaint. How he got there he never knew, but finally he made it. Master Thomas could see how ill he was and told Fred that he could stay there for the night, but that he must go back the next day. He made excuses for Mr. Covey, saying that he was a good man who went to church every Sunday and that Fred belonged to him for a year.

When he got back, Mr. Covey made him go into the stable. He was going to tie him up to an overhead rafter and whip him. Fred's anger gave him a surge of strength, and he got the better of Mr. Covey, who called to Bill, another slave, to come and help him. But Bill said he was hired to work, not to help whip another slave. Then Fred fought as he had never fought before. And he won!

When he wrote about it years later, he said: "I felt as I had never felt before. My long-crushed spirit rose, cowardice departed, bold defiance took its place. I now realised that however long I might remain a slave in form, the day had passed when I could be a slave in fact."

Afterwards he wondered why Mr. Covey did not have him publicly flogged for raising his hand against a white man. Could it be because he was known as a 'negro breaker' and it would not do him any good if everyone knew that a

Chapter 4. His first attempt to Escape

On January 1st 1834, Fred was sent to another master named William Freeland. He was "an educated Southern gentleman" who treated his slaves better than any of the other owners. Fred had not been with him long before he was able to set up a Sunday School to teach a group of the other slaves to read the Bible. They met in the house of a free black man. At one time Fred had over forty scholars of all ages, men and women. Yet they knew that because it was against the law, they could be arrested at any moment and given thirty-nine lashes! Fred kept up that school for the year that he was with Mr. Freeland. He also spent three evenings a week during the winter teaching the slaves at home.

At the end of the year Mr. Freeland wanted to hire him again, but Fred had now made up his mind that the time had come for him to try to escape. He talked about it to some of the others who had been in his 'class', but they all spoke of the terrible risks they would take. "At every gate which we were able to go through we saw a watchman, at every ferry a guard, on every bridge a sentinel, and in every wood a patrol."

Even so, five of them decided they would risk it. They planned to 'borrow' a boat belonging to a friend of Mr. Freeland. His name was William Hamilton and he was an important man in that place. They would row the boat up Chesapeake Bay as far as they could go and then leave it to drift back to its owner. Then at night they would follow the North Star, as the two Irish workmen had told Fred to do when he was a boy.

As it was the Easter holiday, some of the slaves could go to see their relations, but they had to have a 'pass' from their master. Here Fred's handwriting was useful. He forged six passes: one for each of his friends and one for himself. This is what he wrote:

"This is to certify that I, the under-signed, have given the bearer, my servant, full liberty to go to Baltimore and spend the Easter holidays. Written with my own hand", etc.

He signed it with the name and address of William Hamilton.

Alas! An informer, probably one of the group who got 'cold feet', told of the plan. Early on Good Friday they were called to the house for breakfast as usual. As they got there, four white men on horseback rode up and came into the kitchen to arrest them. Fred managed to throw his 'pass' into the fire. He whispered to the others to eat theirs with the breakfast that Mrs. Hamilton had brought them. But it was no use. They were all taken to prison and kept there till the Easter holiday was over, when Mr. Hamilton and Mr. Freeland came to take their slaves away. Fred was kept there a week longer because he was the ringleader. Then Master Thomas Auld came to claim him. He sent him back to his brother Hugh in Baltimore to learn a trade.

He was hired to a ship-builder and put to learn to caulk. In the days when ships were made of wood they had to be caulked with tar to stop the water from getting in through the seams. Fred was a quick learner and he was there for six months. Then he got into a fight with four white apprentices who would not work with him because he was a black slave.

Fred remembered the fight he had had with Mr. Covey and the vow he had made to himself at that time to stand up for himself. So he took on all four of them. But they did not fight fair. They got him to the ground and one of them kicked him in the eye and nearly blinded him. All fifty of the ship's carpenters stood round shouting and egging on the white lads, but not one of them came to help Fred.

With blood pouring down his face and the yells of "Kill him! Kill him!" in his ears, he ran home and told his story to Master Hugh. He took Fred's part and went to complain to the owner of the shipyard. But he said he

could do nothing about it. Mrs. Auld was also sorry for Fred, and for once she acted in the kind way she had when she first met him, years ago. She washed his wounds and bound up his head and treated him as a human being instead of a slave.

After this, Master Hugh, who was the foreman of the shipyard, saw to it that Fred was properly taught the art of caulking. Soon he was able to earn quite a lot of money.

But he could not keep it. Each Saturday night he had to hand it all over to Master Hugh. Sometimes, if Fred made six dollars, Master Hugh would give him back six cents! Fred felt that this was so unfair that he asked if he could work "for hire". This meant that he need not only work for his master but could take on extra work for other people. He still had to give most of the money he earned in this way to Master Hugh, but he was now able to save some for himself each week. He did this with the firm idea in his mind that he was going to escape one day. Finally he decided on September 3rd, 1838. That gave him three weeks to get ready.

Chapter 5. He Reaches New York and Works for the Abolition of Slavery

As the time drew near, he was sad at the thought of leaving his friends. Also, there was the memory of his first failure. But he knew it was now or never. So, on the day he had planned, he left Baltimore and got to New York without any difficulty. In his book he said that he could not tell how he made his escape because it might get others into trouble. Also, it could make it harder for other slaves to escape, since it would make their owners more watchful.

His first feelings on being in New York were of loneliness and fear of being caught and sent back. He was alone in this big city with no money, no food, no home and no friends.

But before long a friend came along. His name was Mr. Ruggles, and he said he had come to help Fred, calling him by his name. He took him to his boarding-house where there were other fugitive slaves. He said that Fred should leave New York soon and go to New Bedford and get work there as a caulker. Also he told Fred to change his name - Frederick Bailey now became Frederick Douglass.

Before he left New York he wrote a letter to a young woman whom he had known and loved in Baltimore. She was black but not a slave, so she was free to join him, and they were married. "Upon receiving the marriage certificate from Mr. Ruggles, and a five dollar bill, he shouldered one part of their luggage and Anna took up the other and they set out forthwith to take up passage on board a steamship on their way to New Bedford."

He found work on the third day after they got there, and this is what he wrote about it:

"It was new, dirty, and hard work for me but I went at it with a glad heart and willing hand. I was now my own master. It was the first work, the reward of which was to be entirely my own. No Master Hugh to take it from me. I worked that day with a pleasure I had never before experienced. I was at work for myself and my newly-married wife."

He gave up caulking because, even here, the white caulkers would not work with a black man. So he turned his hand to anything. He wrote: "There was no work too hard, none too dirty. I was ready to saw wood, shovel coal, carry the hod, sweep the chimney or roll oil casks - all of which I did for nearly three years in New Bedford before I became known in the Anti-Slavery world."

He read about the Anti-Slavery Society in a paper called "The Liberator". When he could afford to buy it, he read this paper as it came out each week. Then he began to go to meetings, but at first did not take an active part because he felt that what he had to say "was said so much better by others". However, when attending an Anti-Slavery Convention at Nantucket on August 11th 1841, he felt strongly moved to speak and was urged to do so by a man who had heard him speaking in the black people's meeting in New Bedford. At first he was nervous. "The truth was," he said, "I felt myself a slave and the idea of speaking to white people weighed me down." But he soon overcame this and his speech was a huge success. The audience clapped and clapped, and some of them came up to pat him on the back or shake hands.

Very soon afterwards he was asked to become a paid worker for the Anti-Slavery Society, and from then on his time was spent in pleading the cause of his fellow slaves. He worked on committees and attended conventions. He was mobbed and mocked and beaten at times by those who were against the freeing of slaves, but this did not stop him. Then he wrote a book telling about his life as a slave, and when it was published he left the country for fear of being caught and sent back to his master, as he was still legally a slave.

Frederick Douglass

He came to England and lived here for two years, meeting many people who were working for the emancipation of slaves. For the first time in his life he was treated by all as an equal. He also got money from the sale of his book and from those who wished to help him.

In 1847 he returned to America with enough money to buy his freedom. He also used some to set up a newspaper called "The North Star". He published this and wrote articles himself for it to help the cause of abolition. For the next seventeen years he also went about giving lectures, as by this time he had become a very popular speaker with a fine voice and manner.

Everyone, even today, knows the song:

"John Brown's body lies a-mouldering in the grave

But his soul goes marching on."

Fred knew John Brown, who was a white man, but who also worked for the abolition of slavery. They were friends. So when John Brown was arrested and sent to prison, Fred fled to Canada to avoid being sent to prison too. He then came to England once more to give lectures and try to get public help for the slaves in America. Slavery had already been made illegal in England for a number of years.

Then in 1861 came the American Civil War, with North America fighting against the South. Slavery was one of the causes of this war. Frederick, of course, was on the side of the Abolitionists. He helped to recruit two regiments and gave his own sons as his first recruits. At the end of the war, in 1865, when the North won and the slaves were set free, Abraham Lincoln, the President, sent for Frederick. He wanted to ask his advice about Reconstruction: how a new and fairer society could be built out of the ruins of the old.

Frederick the slave boy had now risen to a place of honour in his own country! Later on, he became the United States Minister to Haiti.

Having worked so hard to help in freeing slaves, he now worked with those who were trying to get votes for women. In fact he had been to a meeting about this on the very day that he died, February 20th, 1895. He was seventy-eight years old.

These are parts of a letter which was written by Frederick Douglass to Mrs. Harriet Beecher Stowe, the author of "Uncle Tom's Cabin". Her book had made people aware of the evils of slavery and so helped to bring about its abolition. Some of them gave her a large sum of money to help the slaves now that they were free.

As Frederick Douglass was looked upon as the leader of the black people, Mrs. Stowe asked him to advise her of the best way in which the money could be spent. This is what he wrote:

"My Dear Mrs.Stowe,

You kindly informed me when at your house a fortnight ago, that you planned to do something to help free coloured people in the United States ... To my mind there are three evils from which they suffer; poverty, ignorance and degradation. We must try to lift them out of this state if they are to be out on an equal footing with their white fellow countrymen. How can this be done?

"I feel that the first need is not for High Schools and Colleges. In time we shall need them, but at present they are not our most pressing need. We cannot hope that in a single leap from our low condition, we can reach that of Ministers, Doctors, Lawyers, Editors, Merchants, etc. We shall have these in time. But in their present condition of poverty, parents cannot spare their sons and daughters two or three years at boarding-school or colleges. What we need at present is an 'Industrial College' in which the industrial arts are taught.

"The argument in favour of such a college is that here coloured youths could be instructed to use their *hands* as well as their *heads.* They can be taught how to earn a living after they leave. At this moment I can more easily get my son into a lawyer's office to study law than I can in a blacksmith's shop to blow the bellows and to wield a sledgehammer. If we are denied the means of learning useful trades, we are pressed into the narrowest limits to learn a livelihood. In past times we have been the hewers of wood and drawers of water for American society. Today the coloured men must learn trades; they must find new employment; new modes of usefulness to society.

"We must become mechanics; we must *build* as well as *live* in houses; we must *make* as well as *use* furniture; we must *construct bridges* as well as *pass over* them before we can properly live or be respected by our fellow-men. We need mechanics as well as Ministers. We need workers in clay and leather. We have orators, authors and other professional men, but these only get respect for our race in select circles. To live here as we ought we must fasten ourselves to our countrymen through their everyday needs. We must not only be able to *black* boots, but to *make* them. At present we are unknown in the Northern States as mechanics. We are unknown at any of the great exhibitions of the industry of our fellow citizens. And, being unknown, we are unconsidered."

Tuskegee Institute, which was set up by Booker Washington, and of which he was Principal, was the kind of college that Frederick Douglass had in mind. Here are two tributes paid to Frederick Douglass by Paul Robeson, the great black singer, in his book, "Here I Stand". He calls Douglass "our greatest hero and teacher" and tells how Douglass was offered a home, land, and the means of a good life for himself and his family in England. To this he replied that he must return to America to carry on his fight for his fellow-countrymen there. He had been accused if being un-American, but his reply was:

"I deny the charge that I am against the institutions of America. What I have to say is against slavery and slave-holders. I do not go back to America to sit still, remain quiet, and enjoy ease and comfort ... I glory in the conflict, that I may thereafter exult in the victory. I know that victory is certain. I go, turning my back upon the ease, comfort, respectability which I might maintain here ... Still I go back for the sake of my brothers. I go to suffer with them, to undergo outrage with them, to lift up my voice in their behalf; to speak and write in their vindication; and struggle in their tasks for the emancipation which shall yet be achieved."

It was because Douglass did not give up but kept on fighting for the complete freedom of his people that Robeson regarded him as their first great leader. "Douglass taught us," he said, "that if there is no struggle there is no progress. Power concedes nothing without demand. It never did and never will."

An abridged and simplified version by Marie Stuart (Tyrwhitt) of "Narrative of the Life of Frederick Douglass, an American Slave." Written by himself, 1845.